To Antonio  Davis

From His Godmother
    Sheila Evans

on his 4th birthday
with love

The Old Testament
in Pictures for Little Eyes

The Old Testament in Pictures for Little Eyes

by
Kenneth N. Taylor

MOODY PRESS · CHICAGO

The stories included in this book
have been extracted from
The Bible in Pictures for Little Eyes
by Kenneth N. Taylor

2 3 4 5 6 Printing/   /Year 96 95 94 93

OTHER BOOKS BY KENNETH N. TAYLOR
Devotions for the Children's Hour
Stories for the Children's Hour
The Living Bible (Tyndale House Publishers)

Printed in Singapore
Worldwide Co-edition organised and produced by Angus Hudson Ltd., London

Introduction

 VEN LITTLE CHILDREN can understand great truths when told to them in simple words. And when pictures are added, doubly indelible impressions are made that can last forever.

No other book has changed so many lives so remarkably as the Bible. God's Word can be a source of light to childhood's earliest pathways if carefully presented. It can be a Rock to build a life on, even when that life is very small. "Give us a child until he is five years old," some say, "and his character will be formed forever."

It is incredibly important to begin *direct* Bible training at the earliest possible age, in addition to the influences surrounding the child from earliest days in a Christ-honoring home. This book can be read to children of approximate ages 3½ to 6 with great profit. Children of that age can understand with simple trust the great doctrines of God and His dealings with mankind. With simple trust they can accept and always believe what hardened, older minds find difficult.

It is the hope of author and publisher that this book will be a means of establishing little minds in truths from which nothing that will ever happen in the years ahead can shake them, because their trust will be in the Living God and in His Son, Jesus Christ our Lord.

CONTENTS

	Page
God Makes the World	14
Everyone Is Happy	16
God Makes Adam and Eve	18
Adam and Eve Disobey God	20
Cain Kills Abel	22
Noah Builds a Big Boat	24
The Animals Go into the Boat	26
It Rains for Days and Days	28
Noah and His Family Are Safe	30
Proud Men Build the Tower of Babel	32
Abraham Is God's Friend	34
God Gives the Best Land to Abraham	36
God Will Give Abraham a Little Baby Boy	38
Three Men from Heaven Visit Abraham and Sarah	40
God Tests Abraham's Love for Him	42
Rebekah Says She Will be Isaac's Wife	44
Isaac Meets Rebekah	46
Jacob Lies to His Father	48
Jacob Dreams of a Ladder with Angels	50
Jacob Meets Rachel and They Get Married	52
Jacob Wrestles with an Angel	54
God Tells Jacob to Visit His Father	56
Joseph Has a Special Coat of Many Colors	58
Joseph Goes to Find the Sheep and His Brothers	60
The Bad Brothers Sell Joseph	62
Joseph Now Works in Another Country	64
God Takes Care of Joseph in Prison	66

Joseph Tells the King What His Dream Means 68
Everyone Must Obey Joseph 70
Joseph Gives Bread to His Brothers 72
Joseph Takes Care of His Brothers 74
Jacob Blesses Joseph's Two Sons 76
The Children of Israel Need Help 78
Baby Moses 80
The King's Daughter Takes Moses Home 82
God Speaks to Moses from the Burning Bush 84
Moses and Aaron Warn the Bad King 86
The People Mark Their Doors with Blood 88
The King Is Very Sorry He Hurt God's People 90
God's People Begin Their Long Journey 92
God Makes a Path Through the Water 94
The Soldiers Are Drowned in the Water 96
God Feeds the Children of Israel 98
Water Flows from the Rock 100
God Gives the Ten Commandments to Moses 102
The People Pray to a Golden Calf 104
Moses Talks to God 106
The People Bring Gifts to Help Build God's House 108
God Watches over His House at Night 110
The People Forget That God Cares for Them 112
God Is Angry 114
The Snake of Brass 116
God Makes the Donkey Talk 118
Joshua Becomes the New Leader 120
The Runaway Man Is Safe in the City 122
Learning About God 124

Bringing Gifts to God	126
Moses Sees the Promised Land	128
Joshua's Men Are Helped by the Lady	130
God Makes a Way Across the River	132
The Walls of Jericho Fall Down	134
God Keeps the Sun from Setting	136
Gideon Chooses His Helpers	138
Samson Carries the City Doors Away	140
Samson Pulls Down the House	142
Ruth Goes Away with Her Mother-in-law	144
Ruth Works Hard	146
Hannah Prays for a Baby	148
God Answers Hannah's Prayer	150
Samuel Hears God Talking to Him	152
The Messenger Tells Eli Some Bad News	154
Saul Is Chosen to be King	156
David the Shepherd	158
David Kills Goliath	160
David and Jonathan	162
David Finds King Saul Asleep	164
King David	166
The Golden Ark Is Brought Home	168
David Sings to God	170
God Sends Nathan to David	172
Absalom Gets Caught in the Tree	174
Solomon Is a Wise King	176
Solomon Builds a New House for God	178
Solomon Gives Thanks to God	180
Solomon Prays to an Idol	182

The Birds Bring Food to Elijah 184
The Little Boy Is Brought to Life 186
Elijah's Fire Is Lit by God 188
The Chariot Takes Elijah to Heaven 190
God Never Lets the Oil Jar Get Empty 192
The Sick Man Looks for Elisha 194
The Man Is Made Well 196
Elisha Watches the Angels 198
The Little Boy Is King 200
Hezekiah Asks God to Help Him 202
Josiah Reads God's Book 204
The Men Are Sorry for Doing Wrong 206
Whatever Happens Job Still Loves God 208
Job Is Now Well and Happy Again 210
Isaiah the Prophet 212
God Will Make Everything Happy 214
Jeremiah Is Tied Up 216
God Speaks to Jeremiah 218
The King Is Angry 220
God's People Are Taken Away 222
Jonah Runs Away 224
Jonah Is Swallowed by the Big Fish 226
Jonah Preaches to the People of Nineveh 228
Daniel Will Not Eat the King's Food 230
The Hand Writes on the Wall 232
The Men Watch Daniel Praying 234
Daniel Is Put with the Lions 236

The Old Testament
in Pictures for Little Eyes

**W**HEN IT IS NIGHTTIME and the lights are out you know how dark everything gets. You can't see anything. That is how all the world once was. There were no pretty flowers; there were no trees or grass or birds. There were no children either. There was only darkness. God did not want everything to be all dark. He decided to make some people. People could not live in the darkness so God made a beautiful world full of light.

QUESTIONS:

1. *Can you see anything at night when you go to bed and the lights are out?*
2. *Did God want everything to be all dark?*

Genesis 1:2-5

THIS IS THE BEAUTIFUL WORLD God made. How different it is from the cold, dark picture we looked at before! Now the world is warm and bright and pleasant. The animals are playing and everyone is happy. God has made all these things and all of them are very good but there are no people anywhere. God has not made any people. All the pretty things are here but there are no people to enjoy them, so God will make some people to live here.

QUESTIONS:

1. *Can you see a lion in this picture?*
2. *Can you see any people?*
3. *Did God decide to make some people?*

Genesis 1:1

HESE ARE THE PEOPLE God made. Can you see them in the picture? They are behind the flowers in the middle of the picture. Can you point to them? The man's name is Adam. The lady's name is Eve. Adam and Eve did not have a mother and father. God made them out of dust from the ground, and then He made them become alive. God made them happy and good. They love God and God loves them. In the picture you see them looking up toward God. No wonder they are so happy.

QUESTIONS:

1. *What is the man's name?*
2. *What is the lady's name?*
3. *Did Adam and Eve have a mother and father?*
4. *Who made Adam and Eve?*

Genesis 2:7-9

589

ADAM AND EVE are not happy now. Do you know why they are so sad? It is because they have been bad. They did something God told them not to do. God told them they could eat anything except the fruit from one tree. God told them not to eat that one kind but they could eat all the other kinds. The tree was so pretty and the fruit on it looked so nice that Eve wanted to eat it, but God said, "No." Then Satan, who is God's enemy, told Eve to eat it even if God said not to. Eve took the fruit and ate some of it; then she gave some to Adam and he ate it too. Now God is punishing Adam and Eve. He is sending them out of the beautiful garden and they can never come back again.

QUESTIONS:

1. *Who are these two people?*
2. *Where are they going?*
3. *Why can't they stay in the garden?*

Genesis 3:8-13

THESE TWO MEN are Adam and Eve's children. See how big and strong they are! Once they were little children but now they have grown up. Do you see the one with the lamb? His name is Abel. God told them both to bring lambs to give to God, but only Abel is bringing a lamb. Can you see what his brother is bringing? Is he bringing a lamb? God told him to bring a lamb. Is he obeying God? No, he is not. God does not like this, because he is bringing some things from the garden instead of bringing a lamb. This bad brother's name is Cain. Cain got angry with Abel because Abel did what God said and brought God a lamb. And then, do you know what Cain did? He hit his brother Abel and hurt him so much that Abel died. God will punish Cain for killing Abel. Cain killed his brother Abel because he was angry at God. What a terrible thing to do!

QUESTIONS:

1. *Which of these two men is Abel?*
2. *Which is Cain?*
3. *What did God say to bring?*
4. *Point to the one who is obeying God.*

Genesis 4:8-13

T HIS MAN'S NAME is Noah. Can you say his name? I am glad to say that this man loves God very much. He wants to do whatever God tells him to do. He is a good man. God has told him to build a big boat. It is so big that it takes him a long, long time to build it. Can you see the big boat he is building? See how hard he and his sons are working! They are working so hard because God has told him to build the boat and he is happy to do whatever God says. Do you know why God wants Noah to have a boat? It is because God is going to send so much rain that all the ground and the houses will be covered with water, and if he does not have a boat he will die. The waters would go over his head and he would drown, but if he is in the boat he will be safe and dry. God is going to take care of Noah and his family and keep them safe and dry.

QUESTIONS:

    1. What is this man's name?
    2. What is he doing?
    3. Why is he building the big boat?

Genesis 6:13-22

T LAST NOAH'S BOAT is all finished. Can you see the boat in the picture? It is away in the back, over by the sun. See how nice the boat looks! Now it is time for Noah and his family to go into the boat. God tells Noah to take a mother and daddy lion with him into the boat. He tells him to take a mother and daddy bear too. A mother and daddy of every kind of animal are going into the boat because that is what God said. In the picture you can see all the animals going into the boat. Maybe all the other people laughed at Noah for believing that God would make it rain so hard, but Noah didn't care. He believed God and got into the boat. Then God sent the rain.

QUESTIONS:

1. *Where are all the animals going?*
2. *Who told the animals to get into the boat?*
3. *Why did God want the animals in the boat?*

Genesis 7:6-17

**A**FTER NOAH AND HIS FAMILY and the animals all went into the boat God sent the rain. It rained and rained, all day and all night, and for many days and nights. Down and down the rain came until all the flowers and bushes were covered up with water; soon all the houses and trees and people were covered up with the water too. Noah and his family are safe in the boat where God is taking care of them. The animals are safe too. The bird you can see in the picture is a dove that was inside the boat. Noah let it go out to see if it could find a home, but now it is coming back to the boat because of the water.

QUESTIONS:

1. *Where are the flowers and houses?*
2. *Where is Noah and his family?*
3. *Where are all the other people in the world?*

Genesis 8:8, 9

OW HAPPY NOAH and his family are! They are not in the boat any more. Now at last the water has all gone away and the ground is dry again. Now Noah and his family have come out of the boat onto the dry land. They can see the grass again and the flowers and trees. Now the little children can run and play. Can you see what Noah is doing? He is praying to God. God is glad because Noah is praying. God says He will never again punish bad people by sending so much rain to kill them. God put a rainbow in the clouds because of His promise. Do you see the rainbow in the picture? Have you ever seen a rainbow outside your house? Whenever you see a rainbow it is God telling you that He loves you.

QUESTIONS:

1. *Who are these people?*
2. *What are they doing?*
3. *What is that up there in the sky?*

O YOU SEE the high building the men are making? Why are they making this high building? They are making it because they do not like God. They want to make a high building to prove that they are very great. They think that they are greater than God! God does not like this. He will not let them make the building. He will make them talk so funny that they cannot understand each other. They will not be able to tell what their friends are saying. Then they will stop building the tall tower because they cannot talk to each other and cannot tell each other how to help. This building is called the Tower of Babel.

QUESTIONS:

1. *What are the people building?*
2. *Why are they building it?*
3. *What will God do?*

Genesis 11:1-9

HERE IS A PICTURE of a very important man. His name is Abram. Sometimes he is called Abraham. Abraham is a very good friend of God. God loves him and he loves God. God told him to take a long, long trip, to go far, far away and live there the rest of his life with his wife and his helpers and his camels and his sheep and his cows. Abraham said, "Yes," to God. He told God he would go wherever God wanted him to. Abraham loves God. He is God's friend.

QUESTIONS:

1. *What is this man's name?*
2. *What did God tell him to do?*
3. *Did he do what God said?*

Genesis 12:1-9

661

BRAHAM IS TALKING to his friend whose name is Lot. They are talking about where to live. Abraham has many sheep and so does Lot. Sheep eat grass for their breakfast and lunch and supper. There is not enough grass here for Abraham's sheep and Lot's sheep too. Abraham is saying to Lot, "There isn't enough grass here for all our sheep. Only one of us should live here. One of us should go somewhere else to live where there is more grass. You go where you want to live and I'll take my sheep and live somewhere else." Lot is telling Abraham that he wants to live where the grass is long and green and best, so that his sheep will have plenty to eat. He wants the best grass. Lot is being selfish. He wants the best things for himself. After Lot has taken his sheep and gone away, God will give the best land to Abraham. Abraham isn't selfish, so God will give him the best.

QUESTIONS:

1. *Who are these two men?*
2. *What are they talking about?*
3. *What did they decide?*
4. *What will God tell Abraham?*

Genesis 13:5-18

ABRAHAM IS SAD. He is sad because he has no children. He needs a little boy. He talked to God about this. He asked God to give him a son. God tells Abraham to come outside with Him and look up into the sky at night and count the stars. But Abraham can't count them. There are too many to count. God says, "Abraham, I am going to give you a little boy and when he grows up he will have children and pretty soon there will be so many children that you won't be able to count them. You can't count the stars and you won't be able to count all the children and their children that I will give you." Now Abraham is happy because God will give him a little baby boy. God is glad because Abraham believed Him. Abraham knows that God will not fool him. He knows God will do just what He says.

QUESTIONS:

1. *What is Abraham looking at?*
2. *How many children did God say He would give Abraham?*
3. *Did Abraham believe God?*

Genesis 15:1-7

ABRAHAM HAS BECOME very old. See how old he is! Sarah, his wife, is old too. They are too old to have a baby. But God promised that He would give them a little boy. Three men have come to visit Abraham. Can you see them in the picture? When Abraham saw the three men he ran to meet them even though he was so old and the afternoon was so hot. Abraham knew that the three men had come to visit him from Heaven. He asked them to come and eat with him and they did. They had a picnic under the trees. These men told Abraham that Sarah his wife was going to have a little baby. Sarah is laughing because she does not believe that God can give her a baby. But God will do just what He said. Soon God will give a baby boy to Abraham and Sarah. How happy they will be then! The baby's name will be Isaac.

QUESTIONS:

1. *Where did these three men come from?*
2. *What did the three men tell Abraham?*
3. *Why is Sarah laughing?*

Genesis 18:1-15

GOD GAVE ABRAHAM a little baby boy just as He promised. Now in this picture you can see that the baby has grown to be a big boy. He is with his father Abraham and his father is very sorry. Do you know why the father is sad? I will tell you why. It is because God has told Abraham to bring Isaac here and to kill him. God wants to know if Abraham loves God best or loves his boy best. Abraham loves his boy very, very much, but of course he loves God the very best of all. Soon Abraham will take out his knife to kill his dear son. Then suddenly God will call to Abraham and say, "Stop, Abraham, stop! Don't do that. Don't hurt him. Look behind you!" Abraham will look and see a lamb caught in some bushes. "Kill the lamb," God will say. "Don't kill your son. I know now that you love Me." The lamb will die so that Abraham's big boy can come home again with his father. Now the father is glad.

QUESTIONS:

1. *What did God tell Abraham to do?*
2. *Why did God say this?*
3. *Who did Abraham love most, God or his dear boy?*
4. *Who do you love best?*

Genesis 22:1-13

DO YOU SEE the man talking to the nice lady? Do you know what they are talking about? The man is asking the lady where her father is. He wants to talk with her father. The man has come a long way. He lives with Abraham in another country. Abraham told him to go and find a wife for his son Isaac. The man asked God to help him find the right lady. This is the lady God will give to Isaac to be his wife. The man will ask the lady and her father if she will be Isaac's wife and they will say yes. The lady's name is Rebekah. She will be Isaac's wife.

QUESTIONS:

1. *What is the man talking to the lady about?*
2. *Who sent the man to talk to the lady?*
3. *Will the lady go with him to be Isaac's wife?*

Genesis 24:10-26

O.Steinler

HIS IS THE GIRL who said she would be Isaac's wife. Her name is Rebekah. You can see Isaac running toward her. She has come on the camels for a long, long way to be his wife. She has never seen Isaac before, and Isaac has never seen Rebekah before. They are happy because God has given them to each other. Soon God will give them two babies. They will have twins, named Jacob and Esau.

QUESTIONS:

1. *What is this girl's name?*
2. *Who is running toward her?*
3. *What will their children be named?*

Genesis 24:63-67

OW ISAAC HAS BECOME very old, and soon he will die. His two baby boys have grown up now and one of them is kneeling down in front of him. It is Jacob who is kneeling there. Jacob is not a baby now—he has become a big man and his father is very old. Jacob is telling his father a lie. His father cannot see very well because he is so old. He thinks it is his other boy who is kneeling there. He does not know that it is Jacob. The father wants to give some nice things to his other boy, and Jacob says that he is the other boy; so now the father will give the nice things to Jacob. Jacob wants nice things. He tells a lie to get them.

QUESTIONS:

1. *What is Jacob telling his father?*
2. *Why did Jacob tell a lie?*
3. *Who does the father think is kneeling there?*

Genesis 27:1-25

OW JACOB IS TAKING a long walk to another country. His father has told him to go there to find the girl who will marry him. Jacob is tired and is lying down to sleep because it is night. He is having a dream. Have you ever had a dream? Jacob dreams that he sees stairs or a ladder that is so high that it goes right up into the sky. Angels are going up and down the ladder. Then in his dream Jacob will see God standing at the top of the ladder and telling him that many wonderful things will happen to him because God loves him.

QUESTIONS:

1. *What is Jacob doing?*
2. *Where is he going?*
3. *What is his dream?*

Genesis 28:10-16

ACOB IS NOW a long, long way from home. He is in another country. He is helping a girl whose name is Rachel. She is taking care of her father's sheep. While he is talking, Jacob finds out that the girl is a friend. She invites him to come to her house. Her father will be glad to see Jacob. He will let Jacob and Rachel get married. Jacob will live in that country with Rachel. He will not go home to his father for a long time.

QUESTIONS:

1. *What is this girl's name?*
2. *Who is she talking to?*

Genesis 29:1-12

ACOB IS WRESTLING with an angel, but they are not trying to hurt each other. Jacob wants to win so that the angel will give him many nice things. The angel touches Jacob's leg so that he cannot use it very much, but Jacob will not stop wrestling. The angel wants to stop but Jacob won't let him. Jacob is saying, "I will not let you go unless you bless me." Then the angel said he would give him many wonderful things. Afterward Jacob knew that the angel was God. God blessed Jacob and gave him many presents.

QUESTIONS:

1. *Who is Jacob wrestling with?*
2. *What did Jacob want?*

Genesis 32:24-30

**G**OD TOLD JACOB to move to another house with his wives and children. God told Jacob to go home to his father and visit him. Here you can see them taking a long trip to their new home. The children will be glad to see their grandfather. In this picture you can see their father Jacob talking to their uncle Esau. Their father is afraid of Uncle Esau, but Uncle Esau is kissing him. A long time ago their father had been bad and had stolen something from Uncle Esau. They thought their uncle might try to hurt them because their father had done this. But their uncle is very kind. In the picture you can see him hugging their father.

QUESTIONS:

1. *Are Jacob and Esau fighting?*
2. *Why is Jacob afraid of Esau?*
3. *Where are the children going?*

Genesis 33:1-9

THIS BOY WITH THE PRETTY COAT is Joseph. He is talking to his father, Jacob. Jacob loves Joseph very much. Joseph is seventeen years old and is helping to take care of the sheep. His father has given him the pretty coat as a special present because he loves him so much. The little boy is Joseph's brother. His name is Benjamin.

QUESTIONS:

1. *What is the boy's name who has the pretty coat?*
2. *Who gave him the coat?*
3. *Who is the little boy?*

Genesis 37:3

 OSEPH IS GOING for a long walk to find his brothers and the sheep. His father is asking him to go and find them. Joseph is glad to help. He is telling his father, "Good-by." He will find the brothers and the sheep. But the brothers aren't nice. They don't like Joseph because their father gave Joseph the nice coat. They are angry at Joseph. They will try to hurt him. Isn't that too bad?

QUESTIONS:

1. *Who is Joseph talking to?*
2. *What does his father want Joseph to do?*
3. *Will Joseph's brothers be glad to see him?*

Genesis 37:13-27

OSEPH HAS FOUND his brothers. But what is happening to him? Can you see him in the picture? He is the one without a shirt. Two men are taking him away. His bad brothers are selling him. Do you see the man paying money to one of the brothers? The man is buying Joseph. The cruel brothers are happy because they do not like Joseph. Now Joseph will be taken far away to another country. He can't go home to his dear father any more because his brothers have sold him and the men who bought him are taking him away. But God is with Joseph and it will be all right.

QUESTIONS:

1. *Which one in the picture is Joseph?*
2. *Where are they taking him?*
3. *Why is the man giving money to Joseph's brothers?*

Genesis 37:28-36

OSEPH IS IN ANOTHER COUNTRY far away from his home. But God is there with him and everybody likes Joseph very much. He works hard and he always does whatever is right. The man Joseph works for likes him a lot. He has made Joseph his most important helper. In this picture you can see Joseph telling the other men what to do.

1. Is Joseph at his own house?
2. Does everybody like Joseph?
3. What is Joseph doing?

Genesis 39:1-6

OOR JOSEPH! He is in jail. Do you see the bars on the windows so that he cannot get out? He must stay there for a long time. He has not been bad, but someone told a lie and said that he had been bad. But God is with Joseph there in jail. God is taking care of Joseph even when he cannot get out. The other men in the jail like Joseph. He tells them things that are going to happen to them. God helps Joseph know what is going to happen, and he tells the other men.

QUESTIONS:

1. *Where is Joseph?*
2. *Can he get away?*
3. *Is Joseph telling the men what is going to happen to them?*

Genesis 39:20-23

OSEPH IS TALKING to the great king. Everyone is afraid of the king. He has very much money and can tell everyone else what they must do. If they do not do what he says, he will hurt them. But the king is not happy. Do you know why? It is because he had a bad dream last night. He dreamed about some cows. The cows were fat, and some other cows that were thin came and ate up the fat cows! Someone told the king that Joseph could tell about the dream and why the cows did this. Joseph was in jail but the king let him out. In this picture you can see Joseph telling the king about the dream. Joseph says that God sent the dream to the king. God wants the king to know that pretty soon there wouldn't be enough grass for the cows and they would all get very thin and hungry. God tells Joseph about the dream, and then Joseph tells the king.

QUESTIONS:

1. *What did the king see in his bad dream?*
2. *Who is talking to the king about the dream?*
3. *Who told Joseph what the dream meant?*

Genesis 41:1-13

68

HE MAN SITTING DOWN behind the horse is Joseph. All the people are nice to him. They like Joseph. Why do all the people like him? It is because the king has made Joseph his most important helper. Now everyone must do what Joseph says, or else the king will punish them.

QUESTIONS:

1. *Who is the man everyone is looking at?*
2. *Do the people have to do what Joseph tells them?*
3. *Do you know who Joseph's best friend is?*

Genesis 41:14-16, 38-44

ERE IS ANOTHER PICTURE of Joseph. He is sitting on a golden chair. The other men are his brothers. Do you remember how bad his brothers were? Do you remember that they sold him? They have not seen Joseph for a long, long time. They do not know it is Joseph they are talking to. They are afraid of this man because he is so rich and so great. They have come to ask this man for food because they are hungry. These are the bad men who hurt Joseph. They sent him away when he was a little boy. Joseph knows that they tried to hurt him. Do you think that Joseph will give them food? Yes, Joseph loves his brothers even though they were so bad, and he will give them the bread they are asking him for.

QUESTIONS:

1. *Who is the man sitting down?*
2. *Who are the other men?*
3. *Why did they come?*
4. *Will Joseph give them bread?*

Genesis 42:6-8

OSEPH IS TELLING the bad men that he is their brother. These men thought that Joseph was dead, but he is alive and talking to them. God has made Joseph rich and strong so that he can help his brothers and his father now that they are hungry. The brothers were bad to Joseph and made him go away, but God was with Joseph all the time and took care of him. Now Joseph is taking care of his brothers. He loves them anyway, even if they were so bad. Do you know that God loves you, even when you are bad and even when He must punish you?

QUESTIONS:

1. *What is Joseph telling the men?*
2. *Did God take care of Joseph?*
3. *Will Joseph hurt his brothers because they hurt him?*

Genesis 45:1-15

HIS OLD MAN is Joseph's father, whose name is Jacob. Jacob is very, very old now. He knows that God will soon take him away to Heaven. Jacob is talking to Joseph, and to Joseph's two boys. He is asking God to be kind to these two boys. Jacob is blessing the two boys and praying to God about them. He is asking God to take care of them and help them.

QUESTIONS:

1. *Who is this old man?*
2. *Where is he going to go soon?*
3. *Who is he talking to?*
4. *What is he saying to them?*

Genesis 48:9-16

WHAT IS HAPPENING to these people in this picture? They are working very hard. One man is being whipped. A man wants him to work harder, and that is why he is whipping him. These people who are working so hard are God's people. They are called the children of Israel. Does God know what is happening to them? Yes, and God will help them. He will send a helper. In the next picture you will see who God's helper is going to be.

QUESTIONS:

1. *What is the name of these people?*
2. *What is happening to the man?*
3. *Does God know about this?*
4. *What will God do?*

Exodus 1:7-14

SEE THE LITTLE BABY! Why is his mother putting him in the little boat? She is putting him there because the king wants to hurt the baby. The mother is hiding him. The baby's name is Moses. When the baby Moses grows up into a big man, he will make the king of Egypt stop hurting God's people, the children of Israel. The baby will grow up and be God's helper. God is taking care of Moses by telling his mother to put him into the boat. Moses' sister will watch to see that the baby is all right.

QUESTIONS:

1. *What is the baby's name?*
2. *Why is his mother putting him into the boat?*
3. *Will the baby be God's helper when he gets to be a big man?*

Exodus 2:1-4

SEE WHAT IS HAPPENING to the baby Moses! Some nice ladies were walking along and saw the little boat. The lady looking at the baby is the king's daughter. She is the king's big girl. She wants to take the baby Moses home with her and take care of him. She will take the baby Moses to her house and Moses will live there with her. God is taking care of the baby Moses.

QUESTIONS:

1. *Who found the little baby?*
2. *Is God taking care of Moses?*

Exodus 2:5-10

OW THE BABY MOSES is a big man. He is taking care of some sheep. But now God does not want Moses to take care of sheep any more. Instead He wants him to go to help God's people, the children of Israel. God wants to keep the other people from hurting His children with their whips. God is talking to Moses about this. Moses cannot see God talking to him, but he sees a bush that is on fire. The bush burns and burns, but does not burn up. Can you see the fire in the picture? God is in the burning bush and talks to Moses from there. Moses is hiding his face, for he is afraid to look at God.

QUESTIONS:

1. *Where is the baby Moses now?*
2. *Who is Moses talking to?*
3. *Where is God in this picture?*

Exodus 3:1-6

MOSES AND HIS BROTHER AARON are talking to the king. They tell the bad king that God wants him to let the people alone and not hurt them any more. But the king laughs at Moses and Aaron. He will not stop hurting the people. He will hurt them even more. He tells Moses and Aaron to go away and stop bothering him. Then Moses and Aaron say that God will hurt the king if he doesn't stop hurting God's people. All the water in the mud puddles and in the rivers will become blood. Even what is in the glasses on the tables for lunch will become bloody too. God will do this to the king to make him stop hurting His people.

QUESTIONS:

1. *Where is Moses?*
2. *Who is Aaron?*
3. *What are they telling the king?*

Exodus 5:6-19

HO ARE THESE PEOPLE? What are they doing? These are God's people. They are doing what God has told them to do. God said to take the blood of a lamb and put it on the sides of the doors of their houses, and on the board at the top of the door. Why did God want them to put the blood there? God is going to send an angel and in every house that does not have the blood on the door, the oldest boy will die.

QUESTIONS:

1. *What is the man putting at the side of the door?*
2. *Why is he doing this?*
3. *Did the king put the blood on the door of his house?*

Exodus 12:1-13

IT IS THE MIDDLE OF THE NIGHT and outside everything is all dark. In this picture everyone is crying. Do you know why? It is because the king's oldest boy has died. God's angel came and the boy died because there was no blood on the door. God said to put the blood on the door, but the king wouldn't do it. The king is sorry now that he hurt God's people. He is sorry that he did not believe God and do what God said. Now he will quickly send someone to tell Moses that he will stop hurting the children of Israel. He will tell Moses to take God's people out of his country so that God will not kill any more of his people.

QUESTIONS:

1. *Why is everyone so sad?*
2. *What will the king tell Moses now?*

Exodus 12:29-36

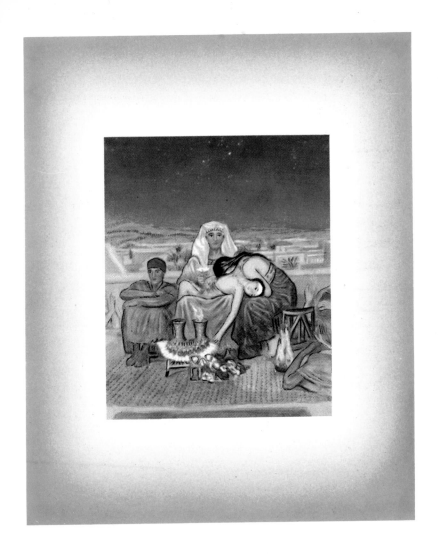

OD'S PEOPLE are going on a long trip, but they do not know where to go. Only God knows where He wants them to go. God is leading them to a good country. God has sent a big cloud that moves along in front of them. They are following the cloud. God moves the cloud and the people go wherever it goes. At night the cloud becomes fire so that the people can follow it through the darkness. That is how God tells them where to go.

QUESTIONS:

1. *How do the people know where to go?*
2. *Who makes the cloud move?*

Exodus 13:21, 22

SEE WHAT MOSES is doing now! God has told him to stand there by the big river. How can all of God's people get across? The water is too deep, and they do not have any boats, and there is no bridge. How can they go across? Moses lifts up his hand, and see what happens! All of a sudden there is a path right through the water so that all of the people can walk through. God has told Moses to do this. God is taking care of His people so that they can get away from the bad king who wants to hurt them. God is very kind to His children. He is kind to you, too.

QUESTIONS:

1. *What is Moses doing?*
2. *What happens when Moses does this?*
3. *Does God love His children?*
4. *Does God love you?*

Exodus 14:21-31

WHAT IS HAPPENING in this picture? Can you see Moses standing there? He is holding up his stick and now the water is coming to cover up the bad king and his soldiers. God pushed the water away so His people could walk through the sea on dry ground. They are safe now. Do you see them there behind Moses? The king chased after them with his soldiers but when he was right in the middle, God let the water come back and the soldiers drowned. You can see the water beginning to cover them up. But God's people are safe behind the cloud that God sent to help them.

QUESTIONS:

1. *How did God's people get through the river?*
2. *What is happening to the soldiers?*

Exodus 14:26-31

ERE ARE GOD'S PEOPLE out in a field. They are the children of Israel. What are they picking up from the ground? I don't think you could ever guess! They are picking up cake that God has dropped down from the skies so that they can pick it up and take it home and have it for their breakfast. There are no stores to go to, to buy food, and so God has sent the food to them. God is very kind to His children. He fed His people this way every morning, and at night he sent birds that tasted like chickens for God's people to eat for supper.

QUESTIONS:

1. *What are these people doing?*
2. *Where did the cake come from?*
3. *What did God send the people for supper?*

Exodus 16:2-6

OSES IS HITTING A ROCK with his stick. Why is he doing this? He is doing this because God told him to. God said that if he would hit the rock with his stick all of a sudden water would come out of the dry rock and there would be a river for God's people to drink from. They were thirsty and wanted to drink, and there wasn't any water, so they started crying about it. They said mean things to Moses. Moses asked God what to do. God told him to hit the rock and water would come out. Now the people have all they want to drink.

QUESTIONS:

1. *Were the people thirsty?*
2. *What does Moses have in his hand?*
3. *How did the water get there?*

Exodus 17:1-6

HIS IS ANOTHER PICTURE of Moses. See what he is carrying in his hands! He has two big pieces of flat stone. These stones have things written on them. God wrote on these stones and gave the stones to Moses. What does the writing say on the stones? It tells what God wants His people to do. It says to love God and obey Him. No one should ever pray to anyone but God. It says on the stones to take care of our mothers and daddies and do what they tell us to do. Another rule God gives is that we should never take anything that does not belong to us. These rules are written on two stones. There are ten rules, so we call these rules the Ten Commandments.

QUESTIONS:

1. *What does Moses have in his hands?*
2. *What are the ten rules called?*
3. *What is one of the rules on the stones?*

Exodus 32:15-19

H, OH, OH! What are these people doing? These are the people of God, but they are praying to a baby cow. Do you see the baby cow in the picture? They have made the cow out of gold and now they are praying to it. These people are disobeying God and making God very sorry. God says we must only pray to Him. These people are praying to something else. Now God must punish these people because they are so bad. Moses is very angry because the people are doing this. He is throwing down the two stones and breaking them.

QUESTIONS:

1. *What are the people praying to?*
2. *Who is the only One we ought to pray to?*
3. *What is Moses doing?*

Exodus 32:1-6

HE BUILDING YOU SEE in this picture is a kind of church. It is the place where the people of Israel can come and pray to God. Moses is there talking to God. There is a big cloud at the door of the church. The Lord is in the cloud and He is talking to Moses. You and I cannot talk to God in a cloud. But we can talk to Him right here in this room. And He sees us even though we cannot see Him.

QUESTIONS:

1. *Where is Moses?*
2. *Where is God?*
3. *What are they doing?*

Exodus 33:7-11

**EE ALL THE PEOPLE COMING!** See what they have in their hands! Some of them are bringing money and some of them are bringing beautiful cloth and some of them are bringing perfume. They are bringing all kinds of things. Do you know why? It is because God has told them that they could bring these things and build a beautiful house for God to live in. They are giving these things to God, and then some of them will help Moses make the beautiful house. The people are happy because they can give these presents to God for His house.

QUESTIONS:

1. *What are the people bringing?*
2. *Why are they bringing these presents?*

Exodus 35:4-29

108

I T IS NIGHTTIME and some of the children of Israel are looking at the beautiful house they have made for God. Is the house on fire? No, it is not on fire, but there is a big cloud of fire there above the house. Do you know who is in the fiery cloud? It is God. God is watching over His house. He is taking care of all the people of Israel in the tents that you can see. Whenever the fire began to move away, then the children of Israel took their tents with them and followed the fire until it stopped. That is the way God told them where He wanted them to go when it was nighttime. In the daytime He sent a cloud for them to follow.

QUESTIONS:

1. *Is the house burning up?*
2. *Who is in the cloud?*
3. *Where do all the people live?*

Exodus 40:34-38

AN YOU SEE what these men are carrying? It is a great big bunch of grapes on a pole. The grapes are so big and so heavy that the men can hardly carry them. They found the grapes far away in another country. God told them to go there. They found the grapes and brought them home for all their friends to see. God wants these people to take a long trip to that other country, where the grapes are so big and live there. But the people are afraid to go. They think the men who live in that other country will hurt them, so they are afraid. They forget that God will take care of them.

QUESTIONS:

1. *What are the men carrying?*
2. *Where does God want His people to go?*
3. *Are the people afraid to do what God says?*

Numbers 13:23-33

OD TOLD HIS PEOPLE to listen to Moses, but some of them said they wouldn't mind Moses any more. God is very angry with these men. God tells everyone to get away from them, because He is going to hurt them. Then all of a sudden the ground opens up and there is a big hole. They fall down into the ground, along with their houses and their friends, and everything that they own. Then the earth closes up again and they are all killed.

QUESTIONS:

1. *Did these men mind Moses?*
2. *What did God do to them?*

Numbers 16:23-35

AN YOU SEE all the snakes in this picture? Do you know why they are biting the people? It is because the people have been bad again. So God has sent these fiery snakes to bite the people, and many of them are dying. These people have come to Moses. They say, "We have been bad. Please ask God to take away the snakes." So Moses prayed for the people and the Lord told him to make a brass snake and put it on a pole. Moses took a hammer and some brass and made a snake. It isn't a real snake; it isn't alive. God tells Moses that anyone who looks at the snake on the pole would get well again. The people in the picture are looking at the brass snake on the pole. Now they will be all right. But if anyone won't look, he will die.

QUESTIONS:

1. *Have the people been bad again?*
2. *How is God punishing them?*
3. *What has Moses made?*
4. *What will happen to the people who don't look at the snake?*

Numbers 21:5-9

116

 MAN IS RIDING ON A DONKEY and there is an angel standing in front of him with a long knife in his hand. The angel wants the man to stop because the man is going to do something bad and the angel doesn't want him to. The man didn't see the angel at first but the donkey did. The donkey is afraid of the angel and stops. The man is angry because the donkey stops. He hits the donkey and tells it to go on. Then the Lord makes the donkey talk, and the donkey asks the man, "Why are you hitting me?" Just then the man sees the angel standing there. The man is falling down on the ground because he is so scared. This man's name is Balaam.

QUESTIONS:

1. *What was the man going to do?*
2. *Can this donkey talk?*
3. *What did it say?*
4. *Why is the man falling off his donkey?*

Numbers 22:21-34

118

OSES IS SITTING DOWN on the rock. He is a very old man now. Soon he will go away to die. He will go away to live with God. He will not be with the people of Israel to take care of them any more. So now God is giving the people another leader. Now Joshua will take care of them. Joshua is talking to the people and telling them what to do. Moses tells Joshua to help the people obey God.

QUESTIONS:

1. *Where is Moses going?*
2. *Who will take care of his people now instead of Moses?*

Numbers 27:18-23

THIS MAN IS RUNNING FAST. Do you see the other man running after him with a big knife? The first man is running into the city. He was chopping some wood with an axe and had an accident. His axe hit a man who was standing near and the man died. Then he started running away to this city and the other man chased him. You can see that he is all tired out. But now he comes to the city and the other man cannot hurt him here. God made this city so that people could run there and be safe. Now he is safe.

QUESTIONS:

1. *Why is the man running?*
2. *Where is he going?*
3. *Will he be all right now that he is in the city?*
4. *Can the man with the knife hurt him now?*

Numbers 35:9-32

 N THIS PICTURE you can see one of God's people talking to his family. He is telling them about God. He wants them to know how good God is to him and how kind God is. He is teaching his children about God so that when they grow up they will always want to do whatever God says. He wants his children to love and obey God even now while they are still young. God always wants fathers and mothers to tell their little children about the Lord Jesus. That is why I am reading these good stories to you—so that you will know more about God.

QUESTIONS:

1. *What is the man telling his family?*
2. *When you become grown up, what will you tell your children?*

Deuteronomy 6:7-14

HESE PEOPLE are bringing gifts to God. They want to give them to God because they are so glad God has been kind to them. The grapes are from their own gardens. Do you see the baskets of grapes? See how many there are! They are taking the first of these grapes and are bringing them to God's house for the priest or minister to use. They will give some to poor people who do not have enough to eat.

QUESTIONS:

1. *What is in the basket?*
2. *Where is the man taking it?*
3. *Why does he want to give the grapes to God?*

Deuteronomy 26:1-11

 OSES IS ON A MOUNTAIN. He is standing on the top of the mountain. He is looking over to the country that God will give to the children of Israel. Moses cannot go there because once he did not mind God. God said that he would have to be punished by not getting to go to the nice country. But God will let him see the promised land. God is showing it to him now. God tells Moses to come up to this mountain so that he can look at it. In a little while Moses will die and God Himself will put Moses' body into the ground. But Moses will go to live with God while his body is there in the ground.

QUESTIONS:

1. *Where is Moses looking?*
2. *Will Moses go to the country where he is looking?*
3. *What is going to happen to Moses?*

Deuteronomy 34:1-12

IT IS NIGHT OUTSIDE. A man is climbing down from a high window. Soon another man will come down too. A lady is helping them. These two men do not live here. They live in another country. They live with Joshua and God's people. God told them to come here and see this city. The name of the city is Jericho. When these two men came to the city, the people who lived there tried to catch them, but the lady is helping them get away. God will be kind to the lady because she is helping these two men.

QUESTIONS:

1. *Do these two men live here?*
2. *Did God tell them to come?*
3. *What did the people try to do to them?*
4. *Who helped them get away?*

Joshua 2:1-15

731

 OD IS DOING A WONDERFUL THING for His children. He wants them to go across the river to the land He said He would give them. There is no bridge for them to go across, and no boat, and the water is too deep to wade. But God makes a way for them to go across. See how the water is standing up like a wall! Now there is a path through the bottom of the river for the people to walk on. The ground is dry beneath their feet. Look at the priests walking ahead of the people of Israel and carrying God's little house. God is making the water stand up instead of getting the people all wet.

QUESTIONS:

1. *How did the people get across the river?*
2. *What is happening to the water?*
3. *Who fixed the river so the people could walk across the bottom of it?*

Joshua 3:13-17

G OD'S PEOPLE are walking around the big city called Jericho. God has told His people to walk around it every day. They have already walked around it once yesterday. They have walked around it once every day this week. Today God told them to walk around it seven times instead of once. Now the people are yelling very loudly and the priests are blowing their trumpets. The high walls are falling down, and now all of God's people can walk right into the city. The people in the city built high walls to keep them out, but God is knocking down the walls. This is the city where the lady lives who helped the two men climb down the wall. The people of Israel do not hurt this lady when they go into the city because she was kind to them.

QUESTIONS:

1. *What are the people doing?*
2. *What is happening to the walls?*

Joshua 6:1-20

134

**D**O YOU KNOW who this man is? He is Joshua the leader of God's people. God's people are having a great fight with some other people. In the picture you can see all the men fighting. The sun is beginning to go down and it will soon be dark. Joshua and God's people will not be able to see to fight. In this picture Joshua is talking to God about the sun. He is asking God to keep the sun from going down. He wants it to stay where it is so that it won't get dark for a long time. God is listening to Joshua's prayer. There will be no night at all on this day. It does not get dark because God is keeping the sun up there in the sky. God listens to Joshua and doesn't let the night-time come.

QUESTIONS:

1. *Did Joshua want it to become dark?*
2. *What did Joshua ask God to do with the sun?*

Joshua 10:6-15

**HY ARE THE MEN** drinking water? Some of them are putting their mouths into the water and drinking like dogs. Others are putting the water into their hands. They will drink out of their hands. Can you tell which ones will drink from their hands? God told Gideon to tell the men to drink the water. He told Gideon to choose the men who drink out of their hands. Gideon will take these men with him to fight with the people who don't like God. He will send all the other men home. God only wants a few men to go. There will not be enough men, so God will help them. God will help them and they will win.

QUESTIONS:

1. *Did God want Gideon to take lots and lots of people with him to fight?*
2. *What are the men doing?*
3. *Which ones did Gideon ask to go with him?*

Judges 7:2-7

705

THIS IS A PICTURE OF SAMSON. Samson is the strongest man who ever lived. He is strong because God made him that way and helped him. God said that as long as he did not cut his hair he would be strong. Do you see his long hair? Here is a picture of Samson and some heavy doors. They are the doors to keep people from going in and out of the walls of that city he is looking at. The doors are shut, and Samson wants to go out. He does not have the key, so he goes out anyway and just takes the doors along with him! What a strong man Samson is!

QUESTIONS:

1. *What is the man's name?*
2. *Did he have the keys to the door?*
3. *How did he get out?*

Judges 16:3

THE STRONG MAN, SAMSON, has chains on his feet. Can you see the chains? How did they get there? I will tell you. One night when he was asleep some men cut off his long hair. Then Samson wasn't strong any more. The men put chains on him and made him blind by hurting his eyes. But now Samson's hair has grown long again and he is stronger. He asked the men to let him stand by the two posts that held up the house. He is pulling the house down and Samson and the people will all die.

QUESTIONS:

1. *What did the men do to Samson's hair?*
2. *How did Samson get the chains on his feet?*
3. *What happened after Samson's hair grew out again?*

Judges 16:18-30

 HIS DEAR MOTHER is going away. Now she will live somewhere else in another country far away. She is saying good-by to Ruth. But Ruth doesn't want her to go all by herself. Ruth wants to go with her and take care of her. Ruth is kind and good.

QUESTIONS:

1. *Is Ruth kind and good?*
2. *Will she go away from the mother?*
3. *Does she want to take care of her?*

Ruth 1:8-18

598

THIS IS A PICTURE of Ruth. Do you remember how kind she was to her mother? Now she is working hard to get food for both of them to eat. Do you see the wheat in Ruth's hands? She will use it to make bread to eat.

QUESTIONS:

1. *Who is this lady?*
2. *What does she have in her hands?*
3. *What will she do with it?*

Ruth 2:5-17

146

ANNAH IS PRAYING. She is praying because she does not have a baby, and she wants one very badly. She and her husband have come to the church to pray and to give gifts to God. The minister sees her praying. He tells her that God will answer her prayer. God will send her a little baby because of her prayer.

QUESTIONS:

1. *Why was Hannah praying?*
2. *What does the minister tell her?*

I Samuel 1:9-19

148

OD GAVE HANNAH a little baby boy. You can see him in the picture. The little boy's name is Samuel. Samuel was a tiny baby but he grew and grew and now he is not a baby any more. Hannah wants to give her little boy to God. She has brought him to the church to be a helper to the minister whose name is Eli. The little boy Samuel is talking to Eli. Samuel's mother will go home now and Samuel will not see her very much. He will live with Eli and be God's helper.

QUESTIONS:

1. *What is this little boy's name?*
2. *Who will Samuel stay with now?*
3. *What will he do?*

I Samuel 2:18, 19

T IS NIGHTTIME and Samuel has been asleep. Now he is awake. Now he is awake and listening to someone talking. He hears someone calling "Samuel! Samuel!" The little boy thinks that Eli is calling him from the next room. He runs quickly to Eli and says, "Here I am, you called me." But Eli says, "No. I didn't call you." "Who called me, then?" Samuel wants to know. Eli tells him that God was talking to him. Samuel will listen to what God says, and do it.

QUESTIONS:

1. *Was Eli calling Samuel?*
2. *Who was calling him?*
3. *What is Samuel going to do?*

I Samuel 3:1-10

ELI IS SITTING ON A ROCK while a man is telling him what has happened. God's people have been fighting with some bad men called the Philistines. The man is telling Eli that God's people are all running away, and that Eli's two sons have been killed. Now Eli is very sad. The man tells him that God has let the Philistines win the fight. When Eli hears this he falls off the rock he is sitting on, and he is hurt so badly that he dies.

QUESTIONS:

1. *What is the man telling Eli?*
2. *Is he telling him happy things?*
3. *What happened to Eli when he heard about it?*

I Samuel 4:5-18

HE LITTLE BOY SAMUEL is now an old, old man. Samuel is pouring oil on the head of a young man whose name is Saul. God has chosen Saul to be king over His people Israel. See how tall and strong Saul is! See how he is kneeling there in front of Samuel! Samuel is pouring some oil on Saul's head because Saul is going to be the king. It looks like he will make a good king for all of God's people to mind. But do you know something that is very sad? I will tell you what it is. Saul's heart has sin in it. That means that Saul will do wrong things.

QUESTIONS:

1. *What is the name of the young man?*
2. *Is he good?*
3. *Why is Samuel pouring oil on his head?*

I Samuel 9:15-27

HIS FINE YOUNG MAN is David. He takes care of sheep. When a lion came to catch David's sheep, David killed the lion. Can you see the lion lying there under his knee? David is strong and good and God is going to let him be the king over His people. God wants Samuel to pour oil on David's head now, so that David will know that he is going to be the king.

QUESTIONS:

1. *What is the name of this young man?*
2. *Does he take care of sheep?*
3. *Will he become king?*

I Samuel 16:1-13

158

Wm. Bouguereau

 GIANT HAS COME to fight against God's people. The giant's name is Goliath. All the men of Israel have run away from him. They are afraid to fight him because he is so big but David is not afraid. David knows that God will help him. David does not have a gun but he has a sling shot. Do you see it in his hand? He takes some stones and uses his sling shot to throw a stone at the giant. The stone hits the giant in the head and the great Goliath falls over dead.

QUESTIONS:

1. *What is the giant's name?*
2. *What did David hit him with?*
3. *Why were all the other people afraid of Goliath?*

I Samuel 17:38-50

AVID AND JONATHAN are talking together. They are good friends and like to talk to each other. Jonathan is King Saul's son. He is a prince. But Jonathan will never be the king because God has told David to be king. Does this make Jonathan sad and angry? No, Jonathan loves David and he is glad that David is going to be the king. Do you see David and Jonathan talking together in the picture?

QUESTIONS:

1. *What are the names of these two men?*
2. *What is the name of the one who is going to be the king?*

I Samuel 20:4-17

THE MAN WHO IS ASLEEP is King Saul. He has been chasing David. He wants to catch him so that he can hurt him and kill him. Saul does not like David. He knows that God is going to make David king instead of him. Saul wants to keep on being king but God won't let him. David and a friend with a spear find King Saul sleeping. David's friend wants to kill King Saul with the sharp spear. But David is good and he won't let his friend hurt King Saul. David knows God would not like this. David only wants to do whatever God tells him. David minds God.

QUESTIONS:

1. *Can you see King Saul?*
2. *What is he doing?*
3. *Can you see David in the picture?*
4. *What is he doing?*

I Samuel 24:1-12

OW SAUL IS DEAD. David is the new king. The old man is pouring oil on his head. He is doing this to make David a king because that is what God said. Now everyone must mind King David. God told David a long time ago that some day he would be king and now he is.

QUESTIONS:

1. *Who is the king now?*
2. *Did David know he was going to be king?*
3. *What is the old man doing to David.*

II Samuel 2:1-4

AVID IS BRINGING HOME the golden Ark. If anyone looked into the Ark he would die. The Ark belongs to God. David is happy that the Ark is coming. He is walking along in front of it playing on his golden harp. Everyone is happy. God is coming to live with them.

QUESTIONS:

1. *Is David happy?*
2. *What happens to people who open the golden box?*

II Samuel 6:12-19

his is a picture of King David. In the Bible there are many songs that David wrote and played on his harp. In this picture you can see him playing and singing. The music is very pretty and the words are nice because they tell how much he loves God. Some of the words he wrote are:

"The Lord is my Shepherd,
I shall not want.
He maketh me to lie down in green pastures.
He leadeth me beside the still waters."

QUESTIONS:

1. *What is the name of this man?*
2. *What is he doing?*
3. *Where are some of his songs written down?*

Psalm 23

HE MAN WITH THE CROWN on his head is King David. God has sent Nathan the prophet to talk to him. See how he is pointing his finger at King David and how David is afraid. David has done a very bad thing and God saw him do it. God sent Nathan the prophet to tell David that God is going to punish him. David is sorry that he has been so bad and asks God to forgive him. God forgives David but he will punish him very much for the bad thing he has done.

QUESTIONS:

1. *Which of these men is King David?*
2. *Has David been good or bad?*
3. *Who sent the other man to talk to King David?*
4. *Did God punish David for being bad?*

II Samuel 12:1-10

THIS MAN who is getting caught up there in the tree is Absalom. Absalom is David's son. He is a prince because his father is the king. Absalom doesn't want his father to be king any more because he wants to be king instead. God does not like this. God wants David to still be king. Now look at Absalom. He is caught in the tree. His donkey is running away. He has been riding on the donkey but now he will hang there by his hair because it has gotten all tangled up in the tree and he cannot get down. Soon some men will come who do not like Absalom. He will not be able to get away from them and they will kill him. Now Absalom cannot be the king. God does not want him to be king.

QUESTIONS:

1. *What is happening to Absalom?*
2. *Can he be king?*
3. *Did God want Absalom to be king?*

II Samuel 18:9-18

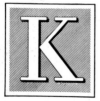ING SOLOMON is telling two ladies what to do. They have come to ask him what to do with the little baby they are holding. Each of the ladies says that the baby is hers. One of them is telling a lie. Which one is it? God tells Solomon how to find out. He says to cut the baby in half and give half of it to each of the ladies. Then the baby's mother says, "No, no, let the other lady have the baby. Don't cut it in half." Then Solomon knows the lady who doesn't want the baby hurt must be the baby's mother. Solomon gives the baby to his mother. God made Solomon very wise.

QUESTIONS:

1. *Did the baby's mother want him to be hurt?*
2. *Who made Solomon wise?*

I Kings 3:16-28

ING SOLOMON built this new house. Do you know who he made it for? It is God's house. It took a long time to build it because it is so nice. Many men have cut down trees and made them into boards and other men cut big rocks and worked very hard. Solomon is glad because he could make this beautiful house for God to live in.

QUESTIONS:

1. *Whose house is this?*
2. *Is Solomon glad?*

I Kings 6:11-14

S.Wilton Lewis Archt
D ALLEMLER

629

OLOMON IS STANDING in front of God's house. See all of the people who have come to have a big party because they are so glad that God's house has been built! Now it is all finished and Solomon is praying. He is standing there with his hands raised before Heaven talking to God. He is thanking God for being so kind to him and to his people and to his father David. He is asking God to take care of them and help them all the time. God is listening. God says he will take care of the people as long as they do what He tells them.

QUESTIONS:

1. *Why have all the people come to God's house?*
2. *What is Solomon doing?*
3. *Is God listening?*
4. *What does God say?*

I Kings 8:22-29

WHAT A SAD THING is happening! Solomon the great king God loves is bad. He is praying to someone else. He is praying to that thing sitting there. A man made it and it is not even alive. It is called an idol. Solomon is praying to it. It cannot hear Solomon's prayer because it is not alive. God in Heaven is watching Solomon. He is very angry about this. God says that now Solomon must be punished. Poor Solomon! Why did he do such a wrong thing? I wish he had remembered to love God and had never prayed to the idol.

QUESTIONS:

1. *Is Solomon praying to God?*
2. *Where is God?*
3. *Will God punish Solomon?*

I Kings 11:1-10

 HIS MAN IS ELIJAH. He is a great friend of God's. Elijah is good but other people tried to hurt him. Elijah asked God to stop it from raining for a long, long time. God listened to Elijah and stopped all the rain. Now the king is angry at Elijah for asking God to do this. Elijah is afraid of the king and runs away and is sitting here by a little river. There is no food here for him and no stores where he can buy it so God is sending him some. The birds are bringing food to him. God is taking care of his friend Elijah.

QUESTIONS:

1. *What did Elijah ask God to do to the rain?*
2. *Why is he hiding?*
3. *How is Elijah getting food?*

I Kings 17:1-7

HIS LITTLE BOY was out playing. Then he began to feel sick. After a while his mother put him into his bed but he didn't get any better. Then the little boy died. His mother asks Elijah to make him alive again. Elijah could not make the little boy alive unless God told him to. Elijah asks God to make the little boy alive and all better again. In this picture you can see what happened when Elijah prayed. The little boy is all right and Elijah is giving him to his happy mother.

QUESTIONS:

1. *What happened to the little boy?*
2. *Who did the boy's mother ask to help?*
3. *What is happening in the picture?*

I Kings 17:17-24

IN THIS PICTURE you can see Elijah praying to God. He is asking God to send fire from Heaven to light the big sticks he has piled on the stones. Do you see the stones and the sticks? Suddenly a great flame of fire comes sweeping down from the sky. God sent the fire because Elijah asked him to. The fire is burning the sticks. How frightened and surprised God's enemies are as they watch. They did not know that God would answer Elijah's prayer. But Elijah is not surprised. He knew that God would hear him. Now all the people know that the Lord is the only God.

QUESTIONS:

1. Where is the fire coming from?
2. Did God hear Elijah's prayer?

I Kings 18:20-39

ELIJAH IS GOING UP to Heaven. His friend Elisha is watching on the ground. They were walking along together when all of a sudden this chariot of fire came down from Heaven and took Elijah up to God. Elisha sees him go. He is picking up Elijah's coat. Now Elisha will not be able to talk to Elijah any more but he can still talk to God. God is with Elisha and talks to him and makes him strong.

QUESTIONS:

1. Who is in the fiery chariot?
2. Where is he going?
3. What is the name of the man who is picking up the coat?

II Kings 2:1-14

DO YOU SEE THIS LADY and her two boys? She must pay some money to a man to-morrow, or the man will take her two boys away from her. He will make them come and live in his house and work hard. Elisha tells her to get all the jars and pans that she can find. He tells her to take the little jar of oil she has in her hand and pour it out into the other jars. She keeps pouring it out but her little jar never gets empty! The oil in it fills all the big jars. See how many big jars she has already filled up. She will sell the oil and get enough money to pay the man so that she can keep her children. God never let the little jar get empty.

QUESTIONS:

        1. *Why was the lady sad?*
        2. *What did Elisha tell her to do?*
        3. *Why doesn't the little jar get empty?*

II Kings 4:1-7

THIS LADY IS WAVING GOOD-BY to her husband. He is going away. He is sick. The girl sitting there told him about God and about God's friend Elisha. The girl said that Elisha could make the sick man well again. He is going away to find Elisha and to ask Elisha to make him well. Elisha will ask God to help and then the man will be all well again. It was nice for the little girl to tell the man and the lady about God. The man did not know about God until the little girl told him.

QUESTIONS:

1. *What did the little girl tell the man and the lady?*
2. *Where is the man going?*

II Kings 5:1-14

194

THIS IS THE MAN we saw in the last picture when he was going away. He has come to ask Elisha to make him well again. He is talking to Elisha. Elisha says to go down to the Jordan River and sit down in it seven times and then he will be well. At first the man doesn't want to do this. He thinks it is a funny way to get well. But soon he goes to the river. One, two, three, four, five, six, seven times he sits down in the river and then he is well again. He brings presents for Elisha to pay for making him well, but Elisha says, "No." Elisha doesn't want his money.

QUESTIONS:

1. *Who is this man who is standing up?*
2. *What does Elisha tell him to do?*
3. *Does Elisha want his money?*

II Kings 5:9-16

ELISHA IS SITTING on top of his house. He is watching some angels up in the sky. They have come to help him and the boy who is there with him. Some bad people want to hurt Elisha so God sends these helpers. They won't let anybody hurt Elisha and his friend.

QUESTIONS:

1. *What is happening in this picture?*
2. *Can we always see the angels?*
3. *Are there any angels here in this room?*

II Kings 6:13-17

HIS LITTLE BOY is seven years old but he is already the king over God's people. God has said that everyone must mind him. He has helpers so that he will know what to do. The little boy's name is Jehoash and he loves God very much. The people are happy because he is their king. When he grows older he will notice that God's house needs to be fixed up and he will fix it. I am sorry to say that when he becomes a big man he won't love God so much. Then he will pray to idols. What a sad thing to happen! When you get big I hope that you will only love God and pray to Him. The little boy in the picture will be very sad after he forgets about God.

QUESTIONS:

1. *How old is the little king?*
2. *Will he still love God when he grows up?*
3. *How old are you?*
4. *Do you want to love God?*

II Kings 11:1-12

ING HEZEKIAH IS CRYING OUT TO GOD for help. He got a letter in the mail from a man who said that he was going to bring a lot of soldiers to catch him. King Hezekiah is very sad and doesn't know what to do. So he comes to God's house to pray and to ask God about it. He is saying, "O Lord, save me and my people! Show everyone how strong You are and that You are our God." God hears King Hezekiah praying. He will send a man soon to tell him that God will help. God will answer Hezekiah's prayer and take care of him.

QUESTIONS:

1. *Why is the king sad?*
2. *Who is he talking to?*
3. *Does God hear King Hezekiah?*

II Kings 19:1-20

HE MAN SITTING ON THE CHAIR is another of God's kings. His name is Josiah. He became king when he was just a little boy eight years old. Now he is grown up into a big man. See how surprised he looks! Someone is showing him a Book that he has found in God's house. It is part of the Bible. The king has never seen the Bible before and did not know what God wanted. Now he will begin to do whatever God says because he has found God's Book and can read it.

QUESTIONS:

1. *Why is the king surprised?*
2. *Where did the man find God's Book?*
3. *Do you have a Book that tells what God says?*
4. *What is the name of the Book?*

II Chronicles 34:18-28

HESE PEOPLE ARE ALL CRYING because they have done such bad things. The man who is talking to them is Ezra. He is one of God's friends so he knows what God wants them to do. Do you know what they have done? These men have married ladies who do not know about God. These ladies want God's people to pray to sticks and stones instead of to God. This is very wrong. Ezra tells the men how bad it is for them to marry ladies who don't love God. God does not want them to marry ladies who do not love Him. Now these men are sorry for what they have done. We should never marry anybody who does not love the Lord Jesus.

QUESTIONS:

1. What did these men do?
2. Can you guess what Ezra is reading to the men?

Ezra 10:1-12

206

THE MAN IN THIS PICTURE, who doesn't have any shirt on, is named Job. He was very rich. He had many sheep and cows. Then he lost all his money and animals. Now Job is very sick and sad. Satan has taken away all of his cows and camels and all of his boys and girls so that he doesn't have anything left. Now he is very, very poor. Job is sorry but he does not blame God. He says, "God, You are good and I love You no matter what happens to me."

QUESTIONS:

1. *What is this man's name?*
2. *What happened to all of his cows?*
3. *Does Job still love God?*

Job 1:1-22

AVE YOU SEEN THIS MAN BEFORE? Yes, this is Job, the man who became so poor and sick and now he is all right again. God has given him more than he had before. He has more cows and more sheep and more money. Job knows that God is good. Job loves God and God loves Job. Do you love God like Job did? Will you do what God says even if God gives you no presents? I hope you will always love God more and more because God loves you so much.

QUESTIONS:

1. *What is the name of this man?*
2. *Has God made him rich again?*

Job 42:10-17

 HIS IS A MAN whose name is Isaiah. God sent him to tell the people what they should do. He is called a prophet. Can you say "prophet"? The people are bad and God sends him to tell them to stop. He says that if they don't, God will hurt their country, and wreck their cities, and burn up their houses. God is sorry when His people sin and do wrong things. God sends Isaiah to help them stop doing what is bad.

QUESTIONS:

1. *What is this man's name?*
2. *What did he tell the people?*

Isaiah 1

 OOK AT THE LITTLE CHILD. Do you see all the animals that are with him? He is touching the cow. A big lion is standing quietly beside him. The lion does not hurt him. Do you see the little lamb, and the black wolf behind the lamb? The wolf does not eat the lamb or hurt it. Some day God will make everything happy. He will make cats and dogs like each other instead of chasing each other. The children will not quarrel and nothing will hurt them. God will make everything want to be kind and gentle.

QUESTIONS:

1. *Will the lion hurt the little child?*
2. *What is God going to do some day to the cats and dogs?*

Isaiah 11:1-10

HIS MAN IS JEREMIAH. Can you say "Jeremiah"? He is one of God's friends. God has sent him to tell the people to be good. The people do not like Jeremiah to tell them this. They want to be bad so they have tied Jeremiah's hands together. They will put him in a room and lock the door so Jeremiah cannot get away. He must sit there all day. People go by laughing at him and making fun of him. Poor Jeremiah! But God is with him and God will punish the people who do this to His friend.

QUESTIONS:

1. *What has happened to Jeremiah's hands?*
2. *Is Jeremiah God's friend?*
3. *Will God help Jeremiah?*

Jeremiah 20:1, 2

**H**ERE IS ANOTHER PICTURE of Jeremiah. Do you remember seeing him in the last picture? Jeremiah is talking to another man who is writing down all the things that Jeremiah tells him to. God is talking to Jeremiah and telling him what to say to the man, and the man is writing it down. He is writing down what God says. He is writing part of the Bible. The Bible is what God says and wants us to know. When the man has finished writing the Book he will read it to all the people, so they will know what God wants them to do.

QUESTIONS:

1. *What is Jeremiah doing?*
2. *Who is telling Jeremiah what to say?*
3. *What is the man doing who is sitting down?*

Jeremiah 36:1-4

I N THE LAST PICTURE do you remember how Jeremiah listened to God and told a man what to write? When it was all written down, God said to take it to the king so he would know what God said. The king read some of it. It said for him to be good and to stop doing bad things. The king is very angry. He does not want to mind God. Oh, oh, do you see what a terrible thing he is doing? He is throwing God's letter into the fire. He is burning it up. He does not want to have God's letter. Oh, how much God will have to punish this king because he will not listen to God or mind Him!

QUESTIONS:

1. *Who is this man?*
2. *What is he doing?*
3. *What will happen to the king because he is doing this?*

Jeremiah 36:19-24

**ERE IS A SAD PICTURE.** It is a picture of God's people being taken away to another country. They are going away from their homes. They want to go home but they can't. The people who are taking them away do not like them and will hurt them and kill some of them. See how sorry the people are! Do you know why this has happened? It is because they are God's people and they are bad, and God is going to punish them. They have prayed to sticks and rocks and the sun instead of praying to God. Instead of spanking them, God takes them away to another country where they don't want to go. In the picture you can see them going away.

QUESTIONS:

1. *Are the people going home?*
2. *Why is this happening?*

Jeremiah 39:1-10

THIS MAN'S NAME IS JONAH. He is running away from God. God has told him to go to a big city and tell the people there to stop being bad. Jonah is afraid to go. He is afraid the people will hurt him if he tells them what God said. So now he is running away instead of doing what God told him to. He is getting on a ship to sail far, far away to another country. He thinks God will not find him there. But nobody can run away from God. Jonah should know that. You know it, don't you?

QUESTIONS:

1. *Where is Jonah going?*
2. *Is he minding God?*
3. *What did God want Jonah to do?*

Jonah 1:1-3

WHO IS THIS MAN swimming in the water? It is Jonah. He was in that boat and a big storm came along. All the men in the boat prayed to God to help them. They asked God to keep their boat from sinking. Then Jonah told them to throw him into the water and the storm would go away. He said he was running away from God and that God had sent the storm to punish him. The men were sad, but they did what Jonah said and threw him out of the boat into the water and now the storm is going away. Jonah is in the water but God won't let him die. He has sent a great fish to swallow Jonah without hurting him. Do you see the fish? After three days this fish will swim over to the beach with Jonah inside and spit Jonah out onto the sand. After that Jonah will do whatever God tells him to.

QUESTIONS:

1. *Why is Jonah in the water?*
2. *What is the fish going to do?*
3. *How long will Jonah be inside the fish?*

Jonah 1:3-17

HERE IS ANOTHER PICTURE of Jonah, the man who ran away from God and was swallowed by a big fish. After the fish had spit him out onto the dry ground, God spoke again to Jonah and told him to go to the city of Nineveh and to preach to the people there. "Jonah," God said, "tell the people who live in Nineveh that they have been bad and I will need to punish them next month." Here in this picture you can see Jonah doing what God told him to. He is telling all the people what God said. The people are listening. They are sorry and afraid. Now they will stop doing bad things because they know God will punish them if they keep on doing them. Now God will not need to punish these people because they are listening to Jonah. Aren't you glad that Jonah did not try to run away again?

QUESTIONS:

1. *What is Jonah telling the people?*
2. *What are the people doing?*
3. *Will God need to punish these people now?*

Jonah 3:1-10

OW I AM GOING TO TELL you a very wonderful story about a boy named Daniel. The king has sent some very good food for Daniel to eat, but Daniel won't eat it. In the picture you can see him telling the two men to take the food away. Shall I tell you why? Daniel doesn't want to eat the good food because the king doesn't believe in God. The king prays to sticks and stones and idols. When the king asks the blessing at the table, he doesn't ask God to bless the food. Instead the king prays to sticks and stones and ugly idols and asks them to bless it. Daniel doesn't want to eat that kind of food, even if it is cake and candy and ice cream. Daniel wants God to be happy, more than he wants to eat. Daniel would rather have oatmeal or soup from God than to have cake from the bad king.

QUESTIONS:

1. *Who is this man?*
2. *What is happening in this picture?*

Daniel 1:3-17

THE KING HAS MANY FRIENDS with him eating lots of good food. But do you see something very strange in this picture? Can you see where Daniel is pointing? Do you see the hand on the wall writing strange letters? No one is there, only a hand. Where does the hand come from? It must be an angel's hand, or perhaps the hand of God that is writing these letters. The king does not know what they mean. Daniel is pointing to the letters and reading them to the king. Daniel tells the king that God is angry and that the king can't be the king any more. God won't let him.

QUESTIONS:

1. *Whose hand is writing the letters on the wall?*
2. *Who is telling the king what the letters mean?*

Daniel 5:1-17

**D**ANIEL IS PRAYING. That is good because God is hearing his prayer and will do what Daniel asks. But do you see the men hiding outside Daniel's door? What are they doing there? They are listening to Daniel. They want to know whether he is praying to God. They say that Daniel must not pray to God. They will hurt him if he does. Daniel knows the men are there listening but he does not care. He prays to God anyway. He would rather pray to God even if the men hurt him.

QUESTIONS:

1. *What is Daniel doing?*
2. *What are the men doing?*

Daniel 6:1-9

HE MEN HAVE PUT DANIEL in with all of these lions. Why did they do this? It is because Daniel was praying to God. The men did not want him to pray so they put him by these lions. They thought the lions would eat Daniel up. Are the lions hurting him? No, they like Daniel. God has sent His angels to take care of him. The angels keep the lions' mouths shut so that they cannot hurt Daniel. He prays to God and God is taking care of him.

QUESTIONS:

1. *Why is Daniel there with the lions?*
2. *Will the lions hurt him?*

Daniel 6:10-23

A larger volume by Kenneth N. Taylor, *The Bible in Pictures for Little Eyes,* includes stories from the Old Testament as well as the New. This classic has been in print for more than thirty years. Today it is published in fifty-four languages and has sold more than 1.5 million copies.